Chakras for Beginners

Chakras - The 7 Chakras Guide On How to Balance your Energy Body through Chakra Healing

Chakras For Beginners

© **Copyright 2016 by Jill Hesson - All rights reserved.**

The contents of this book may not be reproduced, duplicated or transmitted without direct written permission from the author.

Under no circumstances will any legal responsibility or blame be held against the publisher for any reparation, damages, or monetary loss due to the information herein, either directly or indirectly.

Legal Notice:
This book is copyright protected. This is only for personal use. You cannot amend, distribute, sell, use, quote or paraphrase any part or the content within this book without the consent of the author.

Disclaimer Notice:
Please note the information contained within this document is for educational and entertainment purposes only. Every attempt has been made to provide accurate, up to date and reliable complete information. No warranties of any kind are expressed or implied. Readers acknowledge that the author is not engaging in the rendering of legal, financial, medical or professional advice. The content of this book has been derived from various sources. Please consult a licensed professional before attempting any techniques outlined in this book.

Chakras For Beginners

By reading this document, the reader agrees that under no circumstances are is the author responsible for any losses, direct or indirect, which are incurred as a result of the use of information contained within this document, including, but not limited to, —errors, omissions, or inaccuracies.

Table of Contents

Introduction	v
Chapter 1: The Location of the Chakras	1
Chapter 2: Changing your Lifestyle for the Better	5
Chapter 3: Healing of the Chakras	8
Chapter 4: Healing the Throat Chakra	12
Chapter 5: Yoga Poses for the Other Chakras	16
Chapter 6: Stones to Heal Chakras	20
Chapter 7: Cleansing the Chakras	31
Chapter 8: Chakras and Aura	35
Chapter 9: Cleansing Chakras Through Thought and Action	39
Conclusion	41

Introduction

I want to thank you and congratulate you for buying the book, "Chakras For Beginners: Chakras - The 7 Chakras Guide On How to Balance your Energy Body through Chakra Healing". I hope this book can help you understand more about the Basics of Chakras.

Have you heard about Chakras but aren't sure what they are and how they can improve your life? The fact is that Chakras are energy points located throughout the body. When one of points becomes blocked, energy cannot flow as it is intended to flow. Thus, there are certain actions that you can take to heal the flow and make sure that the Chakra is cleared.

This book assumes that you are a beginner. It explores where the Chakras are located and what each one of them does to your sense of wellbeing. When you learn that, you also learn to respect your posture, your interaction with others, and increase your self-esteem levels by making sure that the Chakras are always in perfect alignment.

Although you may be a little doubtful about whether this really works, it has been proven over centuries and is not something new. Those who have been able to keep the Chakras open to the flow of energy that life offers them, tend to be healthy and happy. This book is written to help you to achieve that same level of happiness that is available for all, but that few achieve because of their own inadequacies.

The book explains exercises that you can do to open up problematic Chakras. It talks about things that are important to human beings such as lifestyle and shows you how to gain harmony in your life by balancing your Chakras and to encourage great energy flow. The energy that you gain in your life isn't just a matter of physical activity. Sometimes other things can help you and this book looks at the body as a whole and shows you how to make the most of the life that you have, using the energy flow to keep you enthused about each day of your life. Read through it. Find out where your Chakras are blocked and learn how to unblock that chakra that may indeed be stopping your energy flow. This book targets people who are new to yoga or that have never done it and the exercises contained within the book have been explained for ease of performance. So without any further ado, let us get started!

Chapter 1: The Location of the Chakras

Ever felt pain and pressure in the back of your neck? The chances are that you are stressed and that the chakra, located in the neck region, is taking on all of that negative energy. Negative energy stops you in your tracks and can really make life difficult. This chakra is probably one of the most obvious in the body even to those who know little about the Chakra system. However, do you know where the other Chakras are located? Chances are that you don't. In this chapter, we make you aware of them so that you know from your own experiences that Chakra is giving you problems.

1. The Crown Chakra

2. The Third Eye Chakra

3. The Throat Chakra

4. The Heart Chakra

5. The Solar Plexus Chakra

6. The Sacral Chakra

7. The Base/Root Chakra

The crown chakra is located at the top of the head. The Third Eye chakra is located between the lines of your eyebrows. The throat chakra placement is obvious. The heart Chakra is located in the center of your body at heart level. The Sacral Chakra is just below your tummy button, while your solar plexus chakra is about 3 inches above the tummy button. The base chakra is located at the base of the spine.

You can see that these are represented by colors and symbols each of which have meaning. However, as a beginner, it's more important that you know which kind of problems relate to each of the Chakras, so that you can perform the exercises or activities needed to open up that Chakra in times of need. Let's run through the kind of things that each of these Chakras is responsible for, so that you gain a better understanding. It is not as complex as acupuncture because in acupuncture, there are many pressure points. Thus learning about the Chakras is much easier for the beginner than learning other systems of energy control.

The Crown Chakra – If the Crown Chakra is out of whack, you may be experiencing depression. You may also have problems with your concentration. Any mental blockage of any kind can come from this region. In fact, if you are short tempered because of sounds or the density of light, perhaps it is this Chakra that is out of alignment. In a later chapter, we will talk about balancing the chakra responsible for your lack of alignment, though for now, we merely discuss the illnesses likely to be caused by a blockage in a certain chakra.

The Third Eye Chakra – This is responsible for all kinds of things, including blurred vision, lack of intuitive thought, hearing loss, sinus problems etc., but it doesn't stop there. If you have emotional problems then this Chakra is like to play a part. If you feel the need to exaggerate to gain the attention of others, then this is a weakness that could be accounted for by the blockage of this Chakra.

The Throat Chakra – As we already explained stress can cause this chakra to be blocked, but there are other health issues as well. For example, Thyroid conditions, facial pain or even ear infections can all be caused by the blockage of this particular chakra.

The Heart Chakra – This is an important Chakra when it comes to illnesses that are serious. Lung disease, heart problems and pains in the lower arm can all be attributable to a blockage of this chakra. If you find that your upper back area has problems or your shoulders hurt, this is also likely to be the chakra that is causing that pain. Emotional imbalances may be the cause of this Chakra being out of alignment too and this includes feelings of jealousy, insecurity with relationships or any anger that comes from your relationships with others.

The Solar Plexus Chakra – This chakra is related to digestive problems, gall bladder problems and even chronic fatigue. That feeling of butterflies in the stomach or nervousness when faced by new things comes from this region as well as fears of being rejected.

The Sacral Chakra – If you suffer from urinary problems, this is likely to be the offender. Pains that arise in the lower back area can also come from this chakra, as can liver problems. This chakra is a great chakra to balance because it gives you dynamism and confidence.

The Root Chakra – This accounts for problems below the area where the chakra is located and that can include knee problems, immunity problems, prostate gland problems, sciatica and even illnesses such as constipation or ailments caused by eating disorders. The root chakra also acts as the main chakra to take account of people's feelings of having all of their needs in life fulfilled, such as housing or being able to support oneself. This chakra is likely to be blocked when your living situation feels out of control.

As you can see, we have generalized each of the areas of the Chakras so that you get a clue as to which Chakra is blocked, depending upon the difficulty that you are currently encountering.

Chapter 2: Changing your Lifestyle for the Better

If you are aware that something is unsatisfactory in your life, then you need to look at the way you live your life and see if there are improvements that you can make which will help the chakras to stay aligned. These are simple to rectify and will help you maximize the potential of your body.

Posture
Being aware of your posture is vital to your health. If you are someone who slouches, you will know already that this causes back pain, but it may just be blocking the Chakras and causing other problems that can affect you long term. Keep your shoulders up. Make sure that you get accustomed to sitting straight, with your feet grounded flat on the floor. If you choose to lie down, make sure that your head is correctly supported. Try to avoid repetitive motion strain. In this day and age, people put too much pressure on one part of the body for too long. For example, if you know your posture at the computer is unacceptable, change your chair! Something that can help you with your posture is taking up yoga as this teaches you to move with your breathing so that everything in your body is perfectly aligned.

Breathing
You may not be aware of it, but many people do not breathe correctly. They can cause over oxygenation of the bloodstream by hyperventilating. Control your breathing by breathing in through the nostrils and feeling a pivoting

motion in the gut as you breathe out. Be aware of pollution and avoid its effects by wearing a suitable protective mask when working with materials that may be harmful. In this instance, yoga also helps because you are taught to breathe in the correct way, and shown the posture that you need to maximize the energy gained from your breathing.

Eating

We are prone to eating fast foods on the go and this affects the Chakra because it can upset the stomach and digestive system to such a degree that you become unnecessarily ill. You need to slow down your eating and be more aware of your bodily needs. Never eat in a rush. Sit down and eat and chew your food correctly. This takes time, but you also need to make time so that you can eat in a way that does not upset the stomach. This is the largest organ in the whole of the human body and it is obvious that if you do not respect it, you will block the chakras and will make yourself feel unwell.

Drinking

How often have you told yourself that you will drink more water? We all do it, but how many of us actually act on the good intention. Try to avoid drinking too much coffee and tea because these are diuretics and simply make you urinate more. If you drink water, the body is able to send it to the places that need it and lessen the possibility of muscular cramp, as well as making the Chakras able to allow energy to pass through them.

Medications

Often there is a consequence to taking excess over the counter medications. See your doctor. Have your health checked and stop trying to treat ailments that can be dealt with by a change in lifestyle. Pharmaceutical companies depend upon people self-diagnosing and many of the pills and potions that people buy are not making their lives better. They are simply teaching them to get into worse habits. If you have a cupboard full of medicines that you have bought for all the ailments under the sun, be sensible about which are actually doing you harm. For example, do you need all the extra vitamins and supplements? What about supplying what you need from natural sources like foods and fresh air and sunshine?

In this chapter, we have talked about generalities because everyone needs to take these into account and change bad habits for good ones in order to sustain good health. If you know that you are guilty of doing things that irritate your own condition, be honest about it and change that activity, because until you do, any unblocking of the Chakras will be temporarily halted by bad actions on your part. If you truly want your Chakras to be healed, give them the best chance possible by being more sensible in your life as this will add to the efficiency of the treatments for each Chakra that are mentioned further on in this book.

Chapter 3: Healing of the Chakras

If you suspect that you are suffering from a blockage of one of the particular Chakras, because your ailments seem to align with those stated in the previous chapter, this chapter will help you to deal with being able to heal that chakra. You will need to be aware that you may have to work on exercises that help you to align all of the chakras because it may be a misalignment of more than one chakra that is causing you the problems that you are encountering. In a later chapter, we will explain yoga poses that can help with each of the chakras, but for the time being, let's look at general action that you can take to improve each of the chakras.

Mindfulness – This helps all of the Chakras and is something you can incorporate into your life. Being mindful means living in the moment and that means cutting out thoughts of the past or worries about the future. You can try mindful meditation, as this is very useful. The idea is to think only about the moment that you are in, so if you choose to do this kind of meditation, sit somewhere that you find to be inspirational, so that you are not drawn into thoughts about the past, but are kept present by what you see around you. As you sit with your back straight, you breathe in a very conscious way, feeling the energy coming into and leaving your body. Look directly in front of you and without judging what you see – either in a negative or positive manner – simply observe.

Mindfulness teaches you to be able to go through situations without judgment and thus, your mind path is not altered by what you see. You are present in this moment in time. Observe, do not judge, and move into the next moment. When you eat, for example, use all of your senses. Smell the aroma of the food, taste the textures and flavors and be conscious of every sensation as you eat. Take your time and enjoy it. Mindfulness when doing a task is also useful. If you have a floor to clean, think of nothing but the task and put everything you are into the cleaning process. Don't be made angry by stains that you find. Simply observe them, clean them up and move on.

Mindfulness is useful in relationships. When someone says something that you disagree strongly with, be mindful that this is a passing moment. Hear what they say, acknowledge it but do not judge it. It will make your acceptance levels easier for you to handle and thus relieve you from blocking chakras through negative thought.

Meditation in general
Meditation is always going to be useful to you in all your dealings throughout life. It teaches you a sense of inner peace and you can learn to meditate on your own, although having classes is helpful. Find a place where you will not be disturbed and where you can sit comfortably. Choose a chair that is hard and sit straight with your feet flat on the floor. As you get better at meditation, you may find that you prefer to sit on a cushion on the floor. If this is the case, then cross your ankles by bending your knees. Your hands in both cases should be placed onto your lap, palm upward – your strongest hand supporting the other. For example, if you are left handed, then your left would support your right.

During the course of meditation, you are not permitted to think of anything other than your breathing and the counting you are required to do. If you do think of other things, then you must instantly forgive yourself and dismiss the thought without allowing it to interrupt the flow of your meditation. Believe me, you will have thoughts, as it is natural for people to think about things. When you are more experienced at meditation, you will find that these thoughts begin to interrupt you less and less.

Breathe in through the nostrils – count 7
Hold the breath – count 4
Let the breath out – Count 8
This counts as one.
Breathe in through the nostrils – count 7
Hold the breath – Count 4
Let the breath out – Count 8
This counts as two.

If you think of other things, dismiss the thought and start again at number one until you reach about ten. Then, start again at one and continue for as long as you wish to. You will find that you need to meditate once a day and keep up this routine to get better at it. When you finish your session, take a little time to think about what you can do next time to make your meditation even more effective. Your heartbeat will go down and your blood pressure will lower so taking your time before rushing back into the world is a very good idea. How will this help your chakras? It will help you to get you thinking in a different way that is more spiritual and will awaken your chakras. It will also help you to open up and heal the root chakra, which depends upon posture. When you meditate, you also feel more conscious of your approach to life, which will also help you to heal.

Chapter 4: Healing the Throat Chakra

An entire chapter has been dedicated to this topic because this is the chakra, that when blocked, can really cause distress and even illness. When the throat chakra is blocked, you may find you have trouble swallowing and may also suffer from a lot of nervous tension. This chapter will help you to improve that tension and clear the Chakra energy route.

Chanting – Although you may have heard of chanting, it's quite possible that you have never taken part in it. Chanting is like singing, but it's a question of singing a word with your lips half closed so that you get a tingle on your lips as you do so. This is a great exercise for opening up your throat chakra as well as working on your third eye chakra.

The kind of word that you can use is OM and only you can decide the pitch at which you sing the OM and the amount of time that you can hold your breath as you sing it. Try this first. Breathe in and then on the out breath use the chant. Do it over and over again as this helps you to clear that chakra. You can also use this when you meditate, by incorporating the chant into the outward breath.

Joyful singing – You don't have to be a member of the choral society to enjoy this. Simply find a tune that you enjoy singing and sing it. Make singing part of your everyday life because when you do, you allow the throat muscles to work and this helps to get rid of the pain in the neck area and to open up the chakra so that your pain levels decrease and you begin to feel more relaxed. There are several reasons why this works. While you are concentrating on something as positive as song, your chakra is not disturbed by your insecurities and worries. Try this in conjunction with mindfulness, and you will certainly be on the road to recovery.

Exercise – There is a wonderful exercise that you can do to help clear the throat chakra. Sit on a hard chair and make sure your feet are grounded and touch the floor. Then you need to place the index finger and the middle finger of your right hand onto the left hand side of the top of your head, bending your head to the side. Breathe in deeply and then when you breathe out feel the air rise to the top of your head and tuck your chin in as much as you can. You will feel instant release. Try this exercise several times.

Yoga Poses that will help release the throat chakra
These are poses that you will learn easily in the early days of yoga classes, but they are also exercises you can do alone. For these poses, be aware that the manner in which you breathe matters. When you are told to inhale, do so, and when you move with during an exhalation, be conscious of the two things coming together. In yoga it is the movement and the breath together that help you to achieve movements that would otherwise be difficult.

Legs up the wall pose
This is a great overall exercise that will help you to open up the throat chakra. Lie on a yoga mat or on a firm bed that is up against a wall, because you need to lie as close as possible to the wall and move your legs upward so that

they are parallel to the wall. Your feet need to be square on to the wall and flat as if you are standing on the ceiling above you. Your arms should be stretched out by your side. Stay in this position for about 10 breaths before releasing yourself and lying flat on the floor in your last exhale.

A shoulder stand

For this exercise, lie flat on your back on your yoga mat with your hands by your sides. The legs are lifted into the air so that they form a right angle with the body. Remember, breathe in and move the legs on the exhale. Then take your hands to support your body and lift your torso on the next exhale. Hold this position for several moments before releasing yourself and allowing the body to drop back to the lying down position. Do this several times because with each time that you lift the torso, fresh blood flow to the neck area is possible thus allowing the muscles in the neck to relax.

The supported fish pose

This is a simple pose but one that may make you feel uncomfortable, but you will overcome that feeling as you see the neck area improving. Roll up a towel into a block and lie this block onto the yoga mat. You need to position yourself so that your shoulder blades fall at each side of the block. Then lower your back so that your shoulders are lifted a little. Let your arms drop down at the side and let your head fall back to the mat. This will give your neck the amount of stretch that it needs to open up the chakra. Breathe in and out for about 10 breaths and then as you exhale, lift your body and stretch forward and relax.

Chakras For Beginners

The suggestions made in this chapter should help you with one of the most commonly problematical areas of your body. The neck takes on a lot of stress and strain in this modern world. For other chakras, follow the exercises shown in the following chapter.

Chapter 5: Yoga Poses for the Other Chakras

By now, you will be beginning to understand that your actions can help the chakras to clear a passage for energy to flow through your body. Here are some specific exercises that help in different areas of the Chakra system throughout your body. We will start at the top of the body and work downward. Some exercises will include yoga positions and others will include other things that you can do to improve open up the chakras in question.

The crown and third eye chakras – These are centers that cater for your spiritual wellbeing. We have already suggested meditation, but relaxation is also useful for these chakras. Lying down and breathing correctly while listening to soothing music will help open up these areas. I would suggest that you immerse yourself into the music and that you have a session of about twenty minutes. Remember that relaxation slows down the heart rate and blood pressure and when your relaxation is finished, take your time to get back to speed, instead of trying to get back into your activities too quickly.

It is also a very good idea to be conscious of your energy flow. That means being aware of your breathing. Lie down and breathe in through the nostrils and feel the energy filling your lungs. Hold the breath for a moment and then breathe out, either through the mouth or through the nostrils. The inhale is always through the nostrils. Keep doing this and, as you do so, watch your body pivot as the air goes in and out of the body. Feel the energy and allow your upper chakras to recognize where there are blockages.

The heart chakra – You may have blockages here caused by bad experiences or bitterness. To activate this chakra in a positive way, try to be pleasant to the people around you and to think positive thoughts. Mindfulness can help you to turn your thoughts into positive ones. Many of the yoga poses that are aimed at the heart chakra are too advanced for beginners. However, there are some that are perfectly safe for beginners to try. Don't try advanced exercises unsupervised as this may cause more problems than it solves. The Cat Cow Pose is one of the best for this area of the body, since it stretches the shoulder muscles and allows the heart area to open. To do this pose, you need to be on your hands and knees on the mat. Your hips are always in line with your knees and your hands in line with your shoulders. Now comes the bit you need to understand. You will be lowering your head but you will need to lift your shoulders above your head and use the breathing to achieve the next movements. Pull your shoulder blades inward on the inhale and then outward on the exhale several times before relaxing.

The Solar Plexus and Sacral Chakras – Since these two chakras are in close proximity to each other, we have grouped them together because the exercises suggested will improve the energy flow through both. The first thing that you need to be aware of is that you are eating a variety of foods and are taking your time with meals, so that your digestive system is able to cope well with what you are feeding it. As with other chakra yoga exercises, you will find loads of suggested exercises on the Internet, but be very careful because many are beyond people who have never done yoga before. It is better to do the exercises that are shown here, as these are more suitable to beginners.

The child pose is something that you can do quite easily. In fact, in beginner yoga, this is one position you are sure to learn early. This pose helps all of the chakra, but in particular the lower chakra in the body. For this position you will be on your hands and knees but do make sure that you have sufficient support to make it comfortable. For example a cushion or a rolled up towel may help. Your knees should be spread apart but make sure that your toes on both feet are touching. Breathe in and then on the exhale lift your arms and feel your height reach its maximum pushing up through your crown chakra. Breathe in, and then while you exhale move your body forward so that it touches the ground in front of you. Keep the arms extended and breathe easily, inhaling and exhaling for about a minute. Then crawl back using your hands to support you until you are in the sitting position.

The root chakra – This is a very important chakra as it will determine how secure you are and meditation will help it to become stronger, as will observing basic posture rules that keep the back straight and proud. The relaxation of yoga helps considerably. There are many complex yoga poses that experienced people will be able to do, but for those who are beginners, I would suggest the corpse pose because it is simple and relaxing and will help you to feel more secure in your life. Lie on your back on your yoga mat and let your arms down into the place they find natural at the side of you with your palms facing upward. Your feet should be at shoulder width apart and should point down to lengthen your body. During the course of this exercise, breathe in and feel the energy go down through the spine. Breathe out and think of nothing except that energy leaving your body. The more you are able to put things out of your mind, the more this position will achieve. It is also very good exercise for beginners because it teaches the rhythm of breathing that relaxes the body in the best way possible. As far as other exercises are concerned, try swimming because this is an exercise that will allow your back to stretch without pressure and that helps the root chakra.

You can see from this chapter that you only need to do basic exercises that do not require expertise to improve the flow of energy through the chakras.

Chapter 6: Stones to Heal Chakras

As you know, chakras, or wheels, are invisible vortices that lie within the center of your body. These chakras help you lead a normal and healthy life. But they are prone to blockages, which can cause you to develop illnesses.

One great way of removing these blockages and improving your life is by making use of colored stones.

These colored stones or gemstones are used to fix any blockages that might be present around the chakras and help cleanse the organs connected to them.

There are many colored stones and gemstones to choose from with each one bearing a specific significance. Let's look at the stones and their effects on the different chakras.

Base chakra- Red and Black
The base or root chakra is governed by the colors red and black. Either or both of these can be used to remove blockages present in this particular chakra. The root chakra governs the rest of the chakras and it is quite important for you to keep this chakra as clean as possible.

The stones used to cleanse this chakra are fire red agate and black tourmaline. Both of these are extremely powerful stones and you must ensure that you only use it on your root chakra. You can use either of these and place it right above your root chakra.

Start by lying flat on your back and close your eyes. Place the chosen stone above the area corresponding to the chakra. You can make use of a cardboard pyramid to cover over the chakra and help trap in the energy. You can allow it to stay there for 15 to 20 minutes before slowly removing the pyramid and the stone.

You can do this 3 to 4 times a week or until you feel like all of the blockage has been removed.

Once the blockages are removed, you will start feeling a bit more grounded and reconnect with your inner self.

Powers of Agate
- An agate can help in aligning your soul with your body
- An agate aids in keeping you grounded
- An agate can evoke your emotions and make you quite passionate
- An agate can stimulate your sexuality

Second chakra- Sacral chakra
The second or sacral chakra is governed by the color orange. This chakra deals with your self-esteem and sexuality. A blockage here can affect either or both these aspects.

The second chakra can be cleansed by making use of carnelian or coral. The latter can be quite powerful and help you remove your blockages with ease.

Start by lying down and closing your eyes. You can place either stone above the place corresponding to the chakra and cover it with a pyramid to trap the energy. The energy will keep circulating within the spot thereby removing any negativity.

You must immediately cleanse the stones so that you don't end up using uncleansed stones for your next session.

Powers of carnelian
- A carnelian helps in building self-confidence and self-esteem
- A carnelian assist in taking swift action
- A carnelian assists in purifying the body and chases away bad habits

Third chakra- Solar Plexus
The third chakra or solar plexus is located in the center of your stomach and blockages here can give you digestive problems.

The color associated with this chakra is yellow. The stones used to cleanse this chakra include citrine and topaz.

Sleep flat on your back and close your eyes, keep your legs joined. You can place either of these stones above the area corresponding to the chakra and cover it with a pyramid. Allow it to stay there for 15 to 20 minutes before removing it.

But remember, you must use just one type of stone per session, as they can be quite powerful and clash with each other.

Powers of citrine

- A citrine stone will help in enhancing your overall creativity
- A citrine stone helps in clearing out your negative thoughts
- A citrine will help in enhancing your will power
- A citrine stone aides in helping you reach out to the divine energy
- A citrine stone helps in overcoming life's obstacles
- A citrine stone helps in enhancing stamina
- A citrine stone can be used to improve metabolism

Fourth chakra- Heart chakra
The fourth chakra is the heart chakra and it is important for you to cleanse this chakra in order to prevent the onset of heart disease and other such conditions.

The fourth chakra is associated with the color green. You can cleanse this chakra by using green tourmaline or jade. Both of these are great for your heart chakra, as they will effectively cleanse it.

Sleep on your back and close your eyes. You can place it over the area corresponding to the heart chakra and cover it with the pyramid.

You will experience a great deal of difference in your overall health once you cleanse this chakra.

Powers of Jade
- A jade helps in balancing out the heart chakra
- A jade assist in balancing out emotions
- A jade helps in attracting wealth and prosperity
- A jade assist in increasing overall energy

Fifth chakra – Throat chakra
The throat chakra is located in the center of your throat and deals with voice issues, ear infections etc.

This chakra is governed by the color blue. You can make use of an aquamarine or lapis lazuli.

Lie down on your back and close your eyes. Place the stone in the center of your throat and cover it with the pyramid. Wait for 15 to 20 minutes or until the chakra is clean. Remove the stone and cleanse it immediately.

Once you cleanse this chakra, you will see that your voice has improved and your infections have reduced.

Powers of Lapis Lazuli
- A lapis lazuli helps in acquainting oneself with their inner self
- A lapis lazuli helps in activating your inner conscious
- A lapis lazuli helps in clearing out all the negative energy from the body
- A lapis lazuli helps in aligning your conscious to evoke the divine

Sixth chakra- Third eye chakra
The third eye chakra is quite powerful and can bestow you with great powers. You must try to keep this chakra as clean as possible.

The sixth chakra is governed by the color indigo. This chakra can be controlled by amethyst or purple fluorite.

Lie on your back and place the stone in between your eyebrows. Leave it there for 15 minutes.

Once this chakra is cleansed you will see that your intuition and self-confidence have considerably improved.

Powers of Fluorite
- A fluorite helps in cleaning your thought process
- A fluorite helps in uniting you energies
- A fluorite can help in eliminating dishonesty
- A fluorite assist in harmonizing your brain's activity
- A fluorite helps in controlling vertigo
- A fluorite helps in fixing teeth and bone related issues

Seventh chakra- Crown chakra
The seventh chakra is located inside your head and governs your mental well being. You must keep this chakra clean in order to remain mentally alert.

The crown chakra is governed by the color purple. The stones used to cleanse this chakra include selenite and quartz. You can use either stone to cleanse the chakra and improve your overall health.

Powers of Selenite
- A selenite helps in opening your third eye
- A selenite helps in clearing away negative energy
- A selenite helps in enhancing your awareness
- A selenite helps in carving the way forward and prevents stagnation

Stone mechanism
Each of these stones is extremely powerful and can be used to cleanse the body. They are used to activate the chakras and also balance their energies.

These chakras vibrate at a certain frequency, which helps in balancing out the frequency of the chakras. Once the frequencies match, the chakras start to shake off their negative energies.

The energy centers in the stones match the energy centers in your chakras and together, they vibrate at a certain frequency that helps in cleansing the chakra thoroughly.

As you can see, each chakra can be healed using different stones. The best way to judge the best stone is by trial and error. You can try both and use the one that works well for your body.

Clear quartz
One of the most powerful stones that can be used to cleanse the various chakras is the clear quartz. The clear quartz will work on all your chakras and cleanse them to remove negative energy. The quartz can also be used to cleanse a room. You can place quartz in a bowl and clean out the atmosphere inside the room.

In fact, you will have to make use of a clear quartz to determine which chakra needs to be healed. To do so, you can make use of a piece of quartz attached to a steel chain.

Lie down on your back and start by holding the quartz over your first chakra. The quartz should move like a pendulum if everything is fine with the chakra. But if something is wrong, then the quartz will start to circle and move in a haphazard manner. This is indication if something not being right with the chakra and you are required to cleanse it.

The quartz can also be used to clean the same chakra by placing it on top and covering it with a pyramid. However, this technique will not be as effective as using colored stones that are designed to suit the particular chakra.

But remember, if you think that a chakra is doing well then you don't have to fix it. You might end up affecting its movement and tampering with its energy balance. So it is best to leave a healthy chakra untouched.

Powers of Clear Quartz
- A clear quartz helps in increasing your overall energy
- A clear quartz helps in improving your memory
- A clear quartz helps in heightening spiritual clarity
- A clear quartz helps in opening up all the chakras
- A clear quartz helps in enhancing your conscious mind
- A clear quartz helps in enhances your psychic abilities
- A clear quartz helps in improving the function of your nervous system
- A clear quartz helps in assist in the growth of hair and fingernails

Jewelry
If you don't have the time to perform the chakra cleansing routine using the different stones, then you can also wear

jewelry made using the colored stones. This jewelry will help you remain healthy. But it is best to wear the jewelry close to where the chakra lies. For example, if you wish to fix the root chakra then you can wear a ring containing agate and if you wish to fix the throat chakra then you can wear a pendent made of lapis lazuli.

But make sure that you don't wear two stones that collide with each other. It is important to know what two stones complement each other and which ones do not. You must avoid wearing stones that can clash as they can negatively impact your chakras.

If you feel like there is a surge of energy passing through your body then it is best to check whether you are wearing stones that are colliding with each other.

Buying the stones
Although colored stones are available in a variety of places, it is important for you to know where to buy the stones from; quality stones will help you heal faster as opposed to mediocre ones.

There are many online stores that offer you these stones but it is best for you to read up on their testimonials to see if they are selling your genuine stones. You can also ask around to see if anybody has any suggestions for you.

You will also find stone sets that will contain all the different stones. You can use them individually to fix the different chakras that lie in your body.

If you are not sure about the kit then you can visit a local stone store and consult with the expert there to help you put with the stones.

The price for the stones varies depending on the quality and type of stone. If you wish to buy the best quality stones then you will have to set an appropriate budget.

Remember not to buy stones that are damaged. They can negatively impact your chakras. The stones should be full and free from damage. There should not be any cracks or dents in the stones. The color should be bright and not pale.

If your stone grows pale over a period of time then it is best to replace it with a new and bright one.

Cleaning the stones

It is quite important for you to clean the stones from time to time, especially if you share them with others. The stones can absorb and contain negative energy, which can be transmitted from person to person.

It is best to clean it immediately after indulging in a cleansing session. Here are some ways in which you can cleanse your chakras.

- One good way of cleansing the stones is by placing them under the moon. Keep them there for 3 nights and remove them in the mornings as sunlight can damage them.
- You can simply run them under cold tap water to remove some of the negative energy.

- You can bury them in the ground for a day and remove them the next morning. Make sure you mark the spot where you bury them.
- You can also place them in a bowl containing sea salt. The salt will absorb all the negative energy and refresh the stones.
- Black tourmaline is a very powerful stone and can be used to cleanse the other gemstones. You can place it in a big bowl of water and then place the other stones inside it. The tourmaline will absorb all the negative energy from the other stones.
- Remember not to expose the stones to any kind of heat including sunlight and hot water. Both of these can ruin the color and utility of the colored stones.

Storing the stones

You must store the stones in a velvet bag to protect them from environmental damage. Sunlight can affect your stone sin a negative manner and also change their basic color. You must ideally clean the stones once a month if you are not using them regularly. But if you are, then you must immediately clean them after every subsequent use.

You can make use of a velvet cloth to wipe them after you have cleaned them. As mentioned earlier, it is best to use a different stone for every different family member to ensure that you don't end up transferring the negative energy.

Chapter 7: Cleansing the Chakras

We looked at the different ways in which you can cleanse your aura using the stone and meditation methods. Now, we will look at some techniques that you can use to holistically cleanse your chakras.

Root chakra
As you know, the root or the base chakra is the most important chakra in your body. It, to a large extent, governs the rest of the chakras and is therefore important for you to keep it as clean as possible. As you know, the base chakra is located a little lower than your pubic bone and deals with keeping you grounded or rooted. One natural method of cleansing this chakra and keeping it healthy is by consuming root vegetables. You can pick from the likes of potatoes, beetroots, onions, carrots etc. and incorporate them, as much as possible, in your everyday meals. Another simple technique is to perform mundane activities that will help you remain grounded. This includes performing house chores, sleeping on the floor, having your meals by sitting on the floor etc. All of these will help you improve the health of your root chakra. You can sit in the lotus pose and chant the word "Lam" to release any pent up energy in this chakra.

Sacral chakra
The sacral chakra is located above the navel. The sacral chakra governs the organs located around your stomach. This chakra deals with sexuality. The best way to deal with blockages in this chakra is to address any sexual issues that you have in your life. If you have a partner then you can open up to them and have the issues addressed. You

must also have your sexual organs examined to ensure that you don't have any illnesses. You must also work on your feelings. Talk it out to someone instead of keeping your feelings inside. It is always better to release pent up feelings instead of allowing them to work on your mind. The sacral chakra, when healthy, will help boost your self-confidence and allow you to stave off sexual tension. You can assume the lotus pose and chant the word "Vam" to free up the energy within this chakra.

Solar plexus
The solar plexus is also known as the naval chakra. The solar plexus helps in increasing your power and presence. You can fix any blockages in this chakra by showcasing your management skills. This chakra helps you establish yourself as a leader and the best way to heal it is to take control of a situation and manage others around you. Surrounding yourself with subordinates will help you exercise control over them. The solar plexus, when functioning optimally, will help you remain with lots of self-confidence and allow you to control the various situations that surround you. You can assume the lotus pose and chant the word "Ram" to open up and cleanse this chakra.

Heart chakra
The heart chakra is located next to the heart and deals with your capacity to love and share feelings. Blockages here can mean either an over sensitive personality or someone who is incapable of sharing their feelings freely. It is important to fix this chakra in order to deal with emotional upheavals. In order to free up the heart chakra, you can start by talking out your emotions with the people around

you. As you know, human beings like to express their feelings and share love. You too must vent out any pent up emotions and feel lighter. If you are having trouble communicating your feelings to others then you can consider writing it down and passing the note to the person. They can read it and help you get overcome your fear of expressing your feelings freely. The heart chakra also helps in opening up your mindset and assists in looking at the different situations through a wider lens. You can assume the lotus pose and chant the word "Yam" to open up this chakra.

Throat chakra
The throat chakra is located in the center of your throat. It deals with speech and confidence. Those that have a blocked chakra will not be able to communicate efficiently. The only way to deal with it is by taking up activities that will help you voice your opinion freely. You can join a group where you can discuss your ideologies openly. You can join in a class where you will have the chance to showcase your expertise. This will allow you to develop self-esteem and self-confidence. You can assume the lotus pose and chant the word "Ham" to open up this chakra and deal with any blockages in it.

Third eye chakra
The third eye chakra deals with your intuition. You can heighten your spiritual well being by eliminating the blockages in this chakra. The third eye chakra also helps in improving your overall awareness. To activate this chakra or to remove the blockages in it, you can indulge in a basic form of meditation. To meditate, start by assuming the lotus pose and close your eyes. Now chant the word "Om"

and focus on your inner self. You will be able to see yourself in a different light. You must meditate for at least 30 minutes a day in order to open up this chakra.

Crown chakra
The crown chakra is the topmost chakra and deals with your mental well being. Those with a blocked crown chakra will be prone to depression. The best way to cleanse this chakra is by engaging in activities that will open up your mindset. You must engage in activities that help you stave off stress and anxiety. Improving your social life and taking up yoga will help you clear out the blockages in this chakra.

These form the different activities that you can take up to free up your chakras. Remember that you must always work from down to up. If you think your root chakra is not strong enough then you must not work on your crown chakra. You must first establish a strong base and then move upwards. You will find it easier to open up every subsequent chakra if you work from downwards to upwards.

Chapter 8: Chakras and Aura

Although it is said that the chakras are imaginary vortices, it is possible for you to check their health by looking at your aura.

What is the aura?
The aura is an invisible force field that surrounds all human beings. The aura, much like a rainbow, is made up of 7 colors with each color representing an individual chakra. The colors of the aura will be bright or dim depending on the health of the chakra.

As you know, each chakra has a specific color attached to it and this will show up on the force field that surrounds your body. You can judge the health of your chakras by looking at your aura and determining which chakra needs to be fixed.

The first color of the aura is red, which pertains to the base chakra. This color clings to the skin of the person and has a wide range. Any issue in the first chakra will show on the red color of the aura in the form of gaps and holes.

The second color in the force field is orange and represents the second chakra. This color sticks to the color red and runs along the length of the body on either side. Any issues in the second chakra will cause the orange in the aura to develop gaps or turn black in certain areas.

The third color in the aura is yellow and it sticks to the orange. This color represents the third chakra and any blockages here will cause the orange to develop gaps and holes.

The fourth color of the aura is green and represents the fourth chakra. Any blockages in the heart chakra will show up in the aura in the form of gaps or black patches in the green color.

The fifth color in the aura is blue and represents the third eye chakra. Any blockages in this chakra will show gaps and patches in the blue ring of the aura.

The sixth color in the aura is indigo and represents the sixth chakra. An issue in the third eye chakra will show up in this ring of the aura.

The seventh and last color in the aura is purple. It represents the crown chakra. Any blockages in the crown chakra will indicate gaps and holes in the purple aura.

Importance of the aura
The aura is an important element of life as it helps in determining the overall health of a person. Those with a bright and vibrant aura will be quite healthy and those with a dull aura will have health issues. The aura is predominantly used to zero in on the chakra that needs to be healed in order to improve the overall health of the person.

Once you learn to read the aura, you will be able to tell which area needs to be fixed and what can be done to fix it.

Finding the aura

It is quite simple to find an aura, provided you go about it the right way. To find the aura, start by practicing with an innate object. Like human beings, non-living things also have an aura based on the movement of atoms.

You can start by choosing a book. Make sure that the book has a light color so that you can easily spot its aura. Place it against a light wall and focus on a small point away from the object. Doing so will help you focus on parameters of the object and the aura that surrounds it.

When you look away, you will have the chance to see a bunch of colors that surround the book. They might not be as bright but careful scrutiny will help you look at the individual colors.

Once you perfect it, you can move to other objects such as a tree or a pet. Making them stand in sunlight will help you look at the aura much easily considering auras tend to expand in sunlight.

Once you are able to successfully see the auras, you can move to your own hand. Hold it up in sunlight and focus on an object a little away from it. You will be able to see the various colors of the aura that surrounds your hand.

You can then make a person stand in sunlight and look at their aura. You can make a note of the colors and which ones need to be healed.

Cleansing the aura

Once you find the problem areas in the aura, you will know which chakra needs to be cleansed. You can clean it by adopting any of the chakra cleansing techniques.

You can also use general techniques to clean the aura from time to time. Here is looking at some of the basic aura cleansing techniques.

- You can cleanse the aura by taking a cold shower. Cold shower helps in fixing the aura to some extent as it reduces the negative energy circulating inside the body. You can take a cold shower after returning from work to help wash away the negativity that you would have absorbed during the course of the day.
- You can burn some sage leaves and bask in its smoke. Doing so will help you avail a physical cleanse and eliminate the blockages in your chakras to a large extent.
- You can also use sea salt to rub all over your body as it helps in reducing the blockages to a large extent. But be a little careful as the salt can contain rough granules that can hurt your skin.
- You can also spend some time outdoors and bask in the sun. Sunlight has a positive effect on the aura and spending 20 to 30 minutes will help you fix any issues. You can play outdoor games to help remain under the sun for long.

These form the different activities that you can take up to fix any issues in your aura.

Chapter 9: Cleansing Chakras Through Thought and Action

It is important to cleanse your chakras from time to time in order to lead a healthy life. Let us take a look back at all the different things that you can do to open up your body chakras.

Think positively
The very first step of the cleansing process is to introduce positivity in your life. Start by clearing out all the past experiences and start on a fresh page. It is important for you to focus on what lies ahead of you and then go about improving your life. Remember that positivity has a lot of potential and can help reach into the depths of your mind to help you eliminate negative thoughts. These thoughts are highly capable of blocking your chakras and us a must for you to eliminate them from your system.

Positive people
One way of introducing positive thoughts is by incorporating positive people in your life. If you are surrounded by negativity then you are bound to absorb the same. It is therefore important for you to be in the company of positive people and improve your mindset. If you think there are negative people around you that are causing you to develop negativity then you must try and avoid them at all costs. Once you improve your company, you will be surprised at the results that it has on your chakras and their healing process.

Mindfulness

Mindfulness is a very important activity that you can take up to influence your chakra healing. Mindfulness deals with remaining present in the current moment and then using it to focus on your chakras. You can visualize them opening up and healing themselves completely. These chakras rotate at a certain speed and you can monitor their movement by closing your eyes and focusing on them. You need not be at home or having a leisure time to indulge in mindfulness. You can do it at any place including the office or an outdoor set up.

Meditation

Meditation involves focusing on your mind and breath. This helps in holistically healing the chakras. There are many forms of meditation to choose from and each one has an effect on a different chakra of your body. For example, you can make use of Kundalini meditation to affect all your chakras or use Qi Gong meditation to fix your crown, heart and root chakras. You can choose the type of meditation to adopt based on which chakra you wish to cleanse. But you must dedicate at least 30 minutes a day to the process in order to avail its full benefits.

Physical Cleansing

You must physically cleanse your chakras from time to time using either the stone method or the aura cleansing method. They are both quite powerful and will help you cleanse your chakras from the inside out. Physically cleansing the chakras will also help you keep them functioning better for a longer time. You need not always do it alone and can avail help from others to cleanse your chakras from time to time.

Conclusion

Now that you understand what the chakras are and what they do, you need to read over the chapter that relates to illnesses and ailments again, so that you can take a pretty educated guess and which chakras are blocked at any time. The more you learn about these energy points, the better your health will be because opening up the chakras is something YOU can personally do something about.

The chapter on general lifestyle changes is also vital because if you are lazy in your approach to life, chances are that you will suffer blockages as a result of your life choices. If you can improve what you eat, how you sit and stand and try to incorporate meditation into your life, you will find it natural to respect your body and to keep it in positions that help the chakras rather than hinder them.

Another aspect that we mentioned briefly is your sense of spirituality and purpose. This is quite important and in your dealings with other people, if you try to be friendly and open, you will find that this helps the heart chakra as well as assisting you to become more at peace with who you are.

After you have read the book, try to work out the chakras in your body that may be lacking in their ability to allow energy to pass through them. Once you fix them, this changes your life considerably and you will begin to feel that your life is offering you much reward for your effort. When I began this journey, I was very hesitant to make the first step but trust me, the most important thing you should do is to take the necessary actions. Since healing the chakras and coming to terms with changes in my health and lifestyle, I have managed to work beyond all of my own difficulties and this book has been written to help those people suffering in that way to find peace.

It is not only possible. It is plausible and proven that when you open up these energy points throughout your body, you improve your health, your relationships with others and even the relationship you have with yourself. Thus, the book addresses people with no experience of yoga or meditation and has explained these in a way that can be done by the absolute beginner.

Finally, if you enjoyed this book, then I'd like to ask you for a favor, would you be kind enough to leave a review for this book on Amazon? It'd be greatly appreciated!

Click here to leave a review for this book on Amazon!

Thank you and good luck!

Preview Of 'Yoga: 4-Week Step By Step Guide for Yoga Beginners. Become A Yoga Guru Of Your Own Physical, Mental And Spiritual Self'

Introduction

We live in a world where we feel completely lost and just riding along. We feel as if we just exist without any particular purpose in life. When that happens, anxiousness, stress and depression starts creeping in, and we stop taking care of how we look as well as our health. The result is an unhealthy lifestyle, which may even advance to various health complications. Have you gotten to that point of your life where you feel you need to find your purpose and bring order to your currently disorderly life?

Well, yoga can do all that since it can help you to bring the much needed order in your physical, mental and spiritual life. What do you think yoga is? Do you think of it as simply executing Olympics level gymnastics stunts? Well, yoga is much more than these stunts. This book will introduce you to yoga, what it is all about and how you can start practicing yoga in as little as 4 weeks.

The Basics

"Yoga" is a Sanskrit word formed from a Latin word *'yoke'* meaning to join. From a human perspective, the easiest way to understand yoga is to view it as a union of various

aspects of the human spirit and body such as the physical, mental, and spiritual being.

In simpler language, we can define yoga as spiritual techniques and exercises that are designed to 'join' your body and mind. It also can help you attain oneness with the universe. Yoga also helps you achieve a healthier lifestyle because it facilitates weight loss, improves blood circulation, and boosts your flexibility.

As we shall see later in the book, different yoga techniques and Asanas demand for specific approaches to derive the expected benefits: unification of various aspects of the human spirit.

In this guide, we shall look at yoga from a varied perspective in a bid to help you derive the benefits offered by yoga.

Before we start discussing how to practice yoga, let us look at the benefits you stand to gain by practicing yoga. By looking at these benefits, you will feel inspired to start your 4-week Yoga challenge.

Why Practice Yoga?

Yoga uses various spiritual and physical exercises that bring many benefits to yoga yogis and yoginis (these are the respective names given to male and female yoga practitioners). For instance, yoga is useful for weight loss, building muscles, relieving stress, and strengthening the heart.

Regular practice can also help you achieve inner peace especially if you pair yoga with meditation. If you are looking for a refreshing leisure activity, yoga can still be an interesting exercise you can practice alone or with friends. Whatever reason you may have for wanting to become a yogi or yogini, yoga can deeply connect your mind, body, and spirit, which can help you experience your real self.

Let us detailedly discuss the various benefits yoga has for its practitioners:

1. Boosts Physical Fitness

Yoga uses various poses and stretches; what we call asanas. Research shows that holding asanas for at least 60 seconds can boost your posture and deadlift strength. Yoga can boost balance of strength onto your opposing muscle groups, and help you improve flexibility and range of motion.

The good thing is that yoga poses are simple and can fit everyone ranging from body builders, athletes, the obese, and members of either gender. When practiced properly, yoga reduces stress buildup in the muscles, relaxes you, and prevents possible workout injuries because it improves flexibility.

To benefit from yoga in terms of strength gains, elongated muscles, and boosting physical fitness, its best to adopt yoga as part of your regular workout program. For instance, doing yoga stretches before strength training allows the muscles to freely workout without actually shutting down in response to stretched tendons.

Better still, yoga aids movement through your full range of motion when hitting weights. With a full range of motion, you can build long and full-toned muscles or abs. Physical fitness experts are of the view that stretching yoga poses elongate the protective heath of connective tissues that cover muscles and its cells and repair worn out muscles.

The main reason why yoga energizes and strengthens muscle groups is the long deep breaths, something you have to do as you practice yoga asanas. These deep breaths supply oxygen to the muscles, and boost your ability to focus on workouts.

Yoga can fit into a busy or sedentary lifestyle. Further, some research shows that yoga can heal chronic pain such as migraines. Without much effort, a beginner yogi such as yourself can learn how to make informed health choices and practice specific yoga asanas and techniques aimed at improving your health. This lifestyle coaching can include various aspects like stress reduction, exercising, diet, mindfulness, and other relaxation techniques.

Here Is A Preview Of What You Can Learn From This Book.

- The Basics of Yoga

- Why Practice Yoga?

- How to Adopt Yoga in 4 weeks: A Three Step Approach

- 4-Week Step By Step Guide

Check out the rest of the book by searching for this title on Amazon website.

Printed in Germany
by Amazon Distribution
GmbH, Leipzig